TERRIFIC TESSELLATIONS
COLORING BOOK

DOVER PUBLICATIONS, INC.
MINEOLA, NEW YORK

The cleverly drawn geometric designs in this intriguing book will have you coloring in no time—just choose colored pencils, felt-tip pens, markers, or crayons, and prepare for the ultimate in coloring fun! You'll discover that some of the repeated patterns even vibrate as you look at them. Just choose your starting point in each illustration, and you'll find yourself creating one multicolored masterpiece after another. Enjoy!

Bibliographical Note

Terrific Tessellations Coloring Book, first published by Dover Publications, Inc., in 2014, is a republication of *Ultimate Geometric Designs,* originally published by Dover in 2009. One additional design has been added for this edition.

International Standard Book Number

ISBN-13: 978-0-486-79018-3
ISBN-10: 0-486-79018-5

Manufactured in the United States by RR Donnelley
79018510   2015
www.doverpublications.com

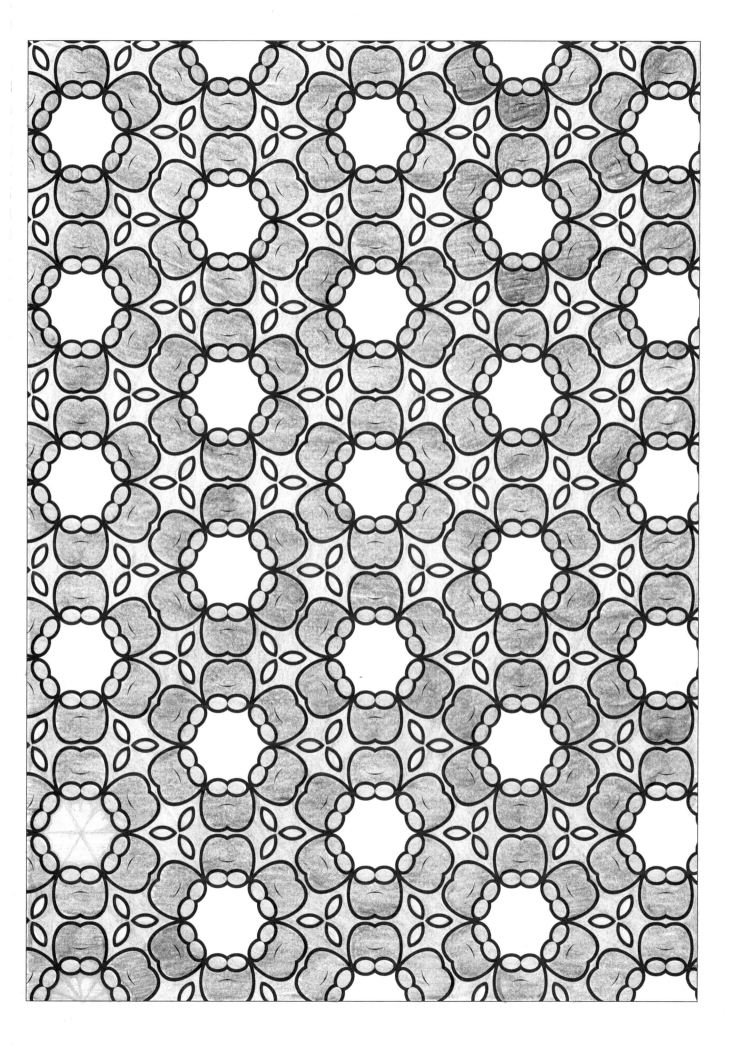

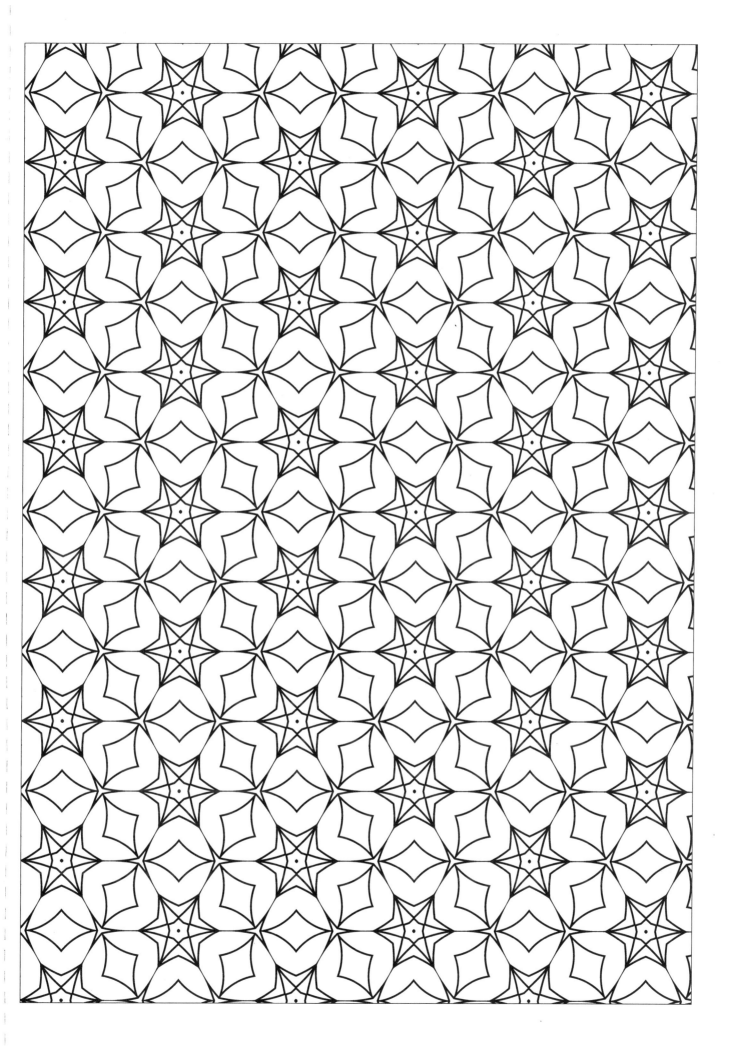

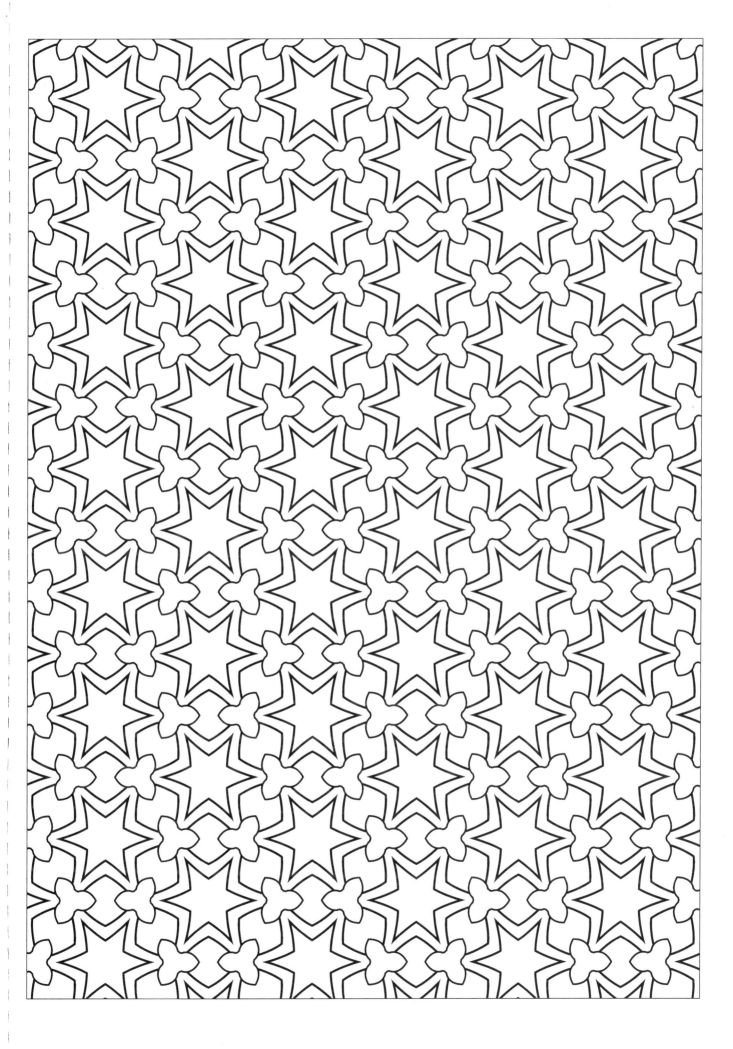